Before The Vows Break

Tales of Triumph Volume II

ISBN-13: 9781734287301

Publisher's Note

Dedication

For wives who have warred before us, wives who war & wives who will war.

For wives who have shared their testimony and those who will be encouraged to share theirs.

For wives who have gone through the fire, those who are in it and those who have yet to enter it.

Had it not been for the Lord who was on our side, who has caused us to triumph in our marriages and over the enemy, we would not be able to share our tests turned testimonies. "... for the accuser of our brethren, who accused them before our God day and night, has been cast down. And they overcame him by the blood of the Lamb and by the word of their testimony..." (Rev. 12:10-11)

Through the pages of this book, you'll read about faith, prayer, strength, courage, and hope from wives who have

"...wrestle not against flesh and blood, but against principalities. Against powers, against the rulers of the darkness of this world, against a spiritual wickedness in high places."

It is our hope that these pages will ignite a fire in you to be the wife who wars that God has called you to be.

Contents

Introduction

Pastor Christopher and Lady Nakia Foster

The Rock Church, Antioch, CA

"Therefore a man shall leave his father and mother and be joined to his wife, and they shall become one flesh."

Genesis 2:24 NKJV

According to Genesis, marriage is the two becoming one. Very seldom do we realize all that this entails. Adam and Eve had the benefit of being connected and growing under the same circumstances and environment. They were devoid of trauma from the past by virtue of being the first one created, and with all of these advantages, they still encountered marital difficulties. When you marry someone, you marry all of them – past, present and future. It's tragic that in our culture we spend more time paying for the ceremony that lasts for a day, instead of investing in the marriage that should last for a lifetime. Therefore, before marriage begins the introspection of singleness should occur.

It was a little over 10 years ago when I (Nakia) had an Abrahamic experience where God called me away from the familiar, my home, family and friends into new unchartered territory. My career was soaring with door after door opening, and my job relocated me to the Bay Area. While things were flourishing for me on the outside, loneliness and depression were growing on the inside. After suffering rejection and heartache from unhealthy relationships, I resolved that my lineage and past were indeed great predictors, love and marriage would never happen for me. So, with that, I dismissed my dream of family and marriage as a fairytale that wouldn't come true and decided I would instead focus on crushing my career goals. My revised life plan: Seize this career opportunity, stay in the Bay Area for 2-3 years and head back to Chicago perfectly positioned for a boss move on the corporate ladder. However, even when you try to throw in the towel on your dreams, God has a way of throwing it back. As destiny would have it, I met and built a friendship with an amazing man shortly after settling into my new home. As our friendship grew my former hope for love and marriage did too. The more I got to know him, the more I saw that he personified all the spiritual and physical characteristics that I prayed for. It made me giddy, nervous, and scared all at the same time. Was this real? Is he too good to be true? I must admit that the pain and rejection of my past made me skeptical. I was waiting on the other shoe to drop but it never did. We were married two years later and shortly after two little bundles of joy came back to back. God had done a quick work and I was now living the dream I thought had fizzled and died. I want to pause right here and insert a little wisdom. Many times, we are praying fervently for God to do a thing for us but those prayers haven't been coupled with the proper level of preparation and the reality is, we aren't ready to handle what we're praying for.

I had no training for being a wife and a mom. Of course, as a Christian single I read books on protecting my purity, serving while waiting, etc. but nothing quite prepared me for being a godly wife. I most certainly didn't see it modeled. My examples were tainted at best. I observed single motherhood, adulterous marriages, passive husbands with aggressive wives or abusive husbands with damaged wives. Nothing I would ever want to follow. Hence why I was forced down the path of OJT (on-the- job training) - stumbling, fumbling, falling, laughing, crying, and overcoming all the odds and obstacles that were stacked against me. And so here I am smack dab in the middle of true irony, as we pen the intro for a book to help marriages and provide insight for those who seek it.

It has been said that if you want to know the purpose, function and intent of a thing, you must go back to its manufacturer, maker, creator. So, it is for us as Christians seeking direction for the God-ordained institution of marriage, the Bible must be our blueprint.

"And further, submit to one another out of reverence for Christ. For wives, this means submit to your husbands as to the Lord. For a husband is the head of his wife as Christ is the head of the church. He is the Savior of his body, the church. As the church submits to Christ, so you wives should submit to your husbands in everything."

Ephesians 5:21-24 (NLT)

Paul describes marriage as a physical manifestation of a heavenly established relationship between Christ and the church. Hence why marriage is under such a vicious attack. The world trivializes it by promoting expensive and elaborate ways to have a 'big day' while ignoring the importance of prayer and preparation for a 'big lifetime.' The law has redefined it by changing the original meaning as outlined by God in His Word. The media attempts to commercialize it by presenting fake, phony, marriages that are based on romance and end in divorce. So, we the church, the body of Christ must fight back in order to preserve, protect and promote the Creator's original intent. It's time for us to declare war in the name of godly marriages!

A war is defined as a struggle between opposing forces, where each side has declared the other as their enemy. It is important to note that the war to preserve, protect and promote godly marriages is a spiritual war and our enemy is not one we can see, and our weapons are not physical ones we can hold. In this war, the enemy disguises himself as our spouse in an attempt to steal, kill and destroy our marriage. So, the first step in winning is knowing your real enemy.

"For we are not fighting against flesh-and-blood enemies, but against evil rulers and authorities of the unseen world, against mighty powers in this dark world, and against evil spirits in the heavenly places."

Ephesians 6:12 NLT

Once we identify our real enemy, we need to prepare for the battles. If you study history, you'll find that wars are comprised of many battles and the War on Marriage is no different. The enemy will use mental, physical and emotional weapons in an attempt to divide and conquer you and your spouse. There's the Battle of Communication, the Battle of Intimacy, the Battle of the Sex life, and the Battle of Infidelity.

The Battle of Communication

Marital misunderstandings occur when there is a lack of communication or miscommunication. Many times, a safe environment for open, honest communication has not been created, resulting in spouses feeling uncomfortable about how they feel, what they want and what they need. You are seething at your spouse because you want them to take more responsibility in the household, sharing the load of housework, kids, bills, errands etc. but you've never taken the time to have a real dialog about your desires. This is an open door for battle and the enemy swoops in.

Your spouse has been short with you for several weeks. They are easily irritated and frustrated and you have no idea why. In the heat of an argument he spews out how your frivolous spending derails every financial goal he tries to set for the future of your family and boom, battle breaks out and the enemy is in. Misunderstandings due to a lack of communication are soil for seeds of marital division, destruction and demise.

The Battle of Intimacy

As women we have a great need for connection and closeness that is birthed out of intimacy. God created us that way. Intimacy is not to be confused with sex (we will address that one next). As a matter of fact, for most women, intimacy is at its purest form when the goal is to connect with our minds and not just our bodies. When the connection and closeness feel forced and contrived, we resort to our defenses - shut down, lash out, rebel and here is where the battle ensues.

The Battle of the Sex Life

Sex is a critical component in marriage. It is designed by God to connect husbands and wives in mind, body and spirit. Perhaps this is why the enemy desires to sabotage sex in marriages. It is imperative that couples are selfless in this area and seek to create an environment where each can discuss freely their desires while the other seeks to cater to and meet the needs of their spouse.

The Battle of Infidelity

Infidelity is one of the most difficult battles to face in marriage. Essentially one or more of the previous battles were lost (communication, intimacy, sex life) and now either one or both spouses have compromised the covenant by having their physical, mental and/or emotional desires met outside of the marriage. The enemy has gained full access into the territory of your marriage during the battle of infidelity and he will bring in a brigade of troops known as unforgiveness, insecurity, guilt, shame, and regret. It will be a hard-spiritual fight and some casualties, such as a loss of trust and intimacy, may occur while trying to reclaim the ground that was stolen but nothing is too hard for God. He is the one that can take what the enemy meant for evil and make it good.

The Bible says, "we overcame the enemy by the blood of the Lamb and by the word of our testimony" (Revelation 12:11 NKJV). As you settle in and glean from the powerful stories and testimonies of the wives in this book, you will find that each has engaged in the aforementioned battles but most importantly you will find that victory comes when you 1) Know your real enemy; 2) Fight every battle spiritually; and 3) Fight every battle with the goal of winning your marriage. Fight on Warring Wife - in the end, your marriage wins!!

But God

Cantres Clark

"They triumphed over him by the blood of the Lamb and by the word of their testimony; they did not love their lives so much as to shrink from death."

Revelation 12:11 NIV

The smile I carry on my face tells a story of triumph; it says that Jesus helped me escape death more than once – a smile that says, as a young child, Jesus allowed me to overcome the mental torment of a heroin addict, as well as being subdued, intimidated and interrogated for hours on end by someone who intended to harm me; and overcome the plot and plans of being a target of a neighborhood kidnapper. Jesus also shielded me from deliberate acts of molestation, which were targeted at me and ultimately failed. Jesus bolted down and mustered my heart to speak up for the next target of molestation – a person whom I loved and still love. My strength in Jesus continued to build as the transgressions against her stopped; these things I saw with my own eyes.

However, there were times when I made it home safe as a child, after fleeing desperately and fearfully from danger – but how I did so cannot be explained in the physical realm. Let's just say it was like my little red Radio Flyer push wagon was miraculously fueled by gas during times of escape. There are so many more childhood incidences, too many to explain in one chapter, that drew my heart toward Jesus. I couldn't comprehend the work that God was doing in me. As an adolescent, I didn't know how to explain that I knew Jesus would never leave me nor forsake me (Hebrews 13:5 NKJV); or that I knew the Lord is my rock, my fortress, and my deliverer; or that God is my strength, in whom I trust; My shield and the horn of my salvation, my stronghold (Psalm 18:2 NKJV). What I said was this, "Jesus has always been sweet to me."

The things that happened in my childhood were catalysts to many behavioral issues that I have overcome; I had to conquer the fear of what drove me to habitually fist fight. If you were coming for me or attempting to shame my personage, I would immediately square up from fear of the opposition getting an oppressive steal. I also had to overcome the fear of sleeping in the dark, for my mind called up many unwelcomed things that happened in dark places. Many times, I slept with a blanket over my head to block out the other worldly atmosphere – I trusted no one except my mother and sister. With the anxiety that I carried into my twenties, one would think that using drugs would compel me. In my early years, I'd rather daydream than ingest mind altering substances as a means of escape, as my previous entanglements with a heroin addict repulsed me. I was angry and horrified by the effects of drug dependence within relationships. Although, the drug life did not influence me, being introduced to the vast world of psychics and clairvoyants did. Knowing future events meant I could take control of my life... Or so I thought. I didn't realize that my behavior had opened the door to the unlit world I desperately tried to flee from. What does this have to do with my marriage? Well, my unresolved trauma reared its ugly head within our marriage in ways that I did not expect. It was not until my mid-thirties, and after being married for several years, that the Holy Spirit set my soul on fire with the revelation of this verse.

"Lord, you prepare a table before me in the presence of my enemies. You anoint my head with oil; my cup overflows." (Psalm 23:5 NKJV). It was at this time that I had to take hold of everything God implanted within me, to withstand and overcome an attack that would leave a scar on my repented heart - a healed scar that God continues unto this day to pour fresh oil over.

It took me a long time to be able to talk about this publicly, because what I am about to share with you may seem peculiar or spooky.

But we press toward the mark, right? They (we) overcame him by the blood of the lamb, and by the word of their (our) testimony; and they loved not their (our) lives unto death (Revelation 12:11 NKJV). Recounting the experiences that led me to war as a wife stem from pure love – a love that desires, then decrees that the chains attempting to threaten our marriages, us as individuals, and our children are broken. I mention children because, to me, taking care of our children is part of being a successful wife.

Sharing our family's stories is my praise and honor to Christ. "To whom be glory forever and ever. Amen" (Galatians 1:5 NKJV).

It was the fight of my life; the familiar phrase "till death do us part" took on a new meaning. It was not a human being who tried to break apart our marriage by killing us, but instead something I call the Poltergeist. Yes, you read correctly. Our family had a three- year battle with this demonic spirit that wanted to trouble, vex, and torment our marriage and family. I wouldn't wish that kind of agonizing fight on anyone. Each of us – my husband, myself, and our two children, all had our own personal fight in this battle, as we had to depend on God's strength during this terrible conflict.

According to our faith, we all had to be strong in the Lord and in the strength of His might. Each of us had to put on the whole armor of God, so that we could stand against the schemes of the devil (Ephesians 6:11 ESV).

My husband and I learned to stand in faith, truth, peace, and righteousness. Our marriage grew to be stronger in the Lord and in His might. We learned that one may be overpowered; two can defend themselves. A cord of three strands is not quickly broken (Ecclesiastes 4:12 NIV).We understand firsthand that our struggles are not against flesh and blood, but against the rulers, against the authorities, against the powers of this dark world and against the spiritual forces of evil in the heavenly realms (Ephesians 6:10-12 NIV). As a wife, it took everything that God has ever placed within me to overcome encounters with a non-physical being who attempted to use our marriage as a bullseye. I use this analogy: I fought with "The Cross, The Sword, and a Stick." The cross represents the blood of Jesus, the sword is the Word of God, and the spiritual stick was everything else that helped me stand; I used the stick to walk when I was in pain. When God gave me strength, I used the stick to draw lines in the sand and stand my ground; and as I continue to be transparent, sometimes I went back to my old ways and swung the stick at others too. But I rested in knowing that all things work together for the good of them that love God, to them who are the called according to His purpose (Romans 8:28 KJV). What I am about to share is my personal fight and struggle during the battle: It is my remembrance of the sword that God asked me to carry in this vicious war. It is how I ran with perseverance the race that was marked out for me within our marriage. It is my recollection of how I was raised up into a Wife Who Wars!

It was in 1994 that I met my sweet husband. He loved me like I had never been loved before. He accepted me with my flaws, and we were inseparable, staying together day in and day out. I was beautiful to him, as he was handsome to me, and he waited on me hand and foot, saying that it was his pleasure. I love my husband because he is strong, loving, intelligent, and unmovable; we got married in 1999. Our wedding was incredible and beautiful. I could go on and on about our remarkable love story, but the essential point I am trying to make is that my husband's unmovable strength was pivotal in winning every one of our battles – including the total knock out that I'll explain in a moment. In 2001, my husband and I decided to move from Antioch, CA, to the Dallas Metroplex.

Our son was 10 months old at the time, and our daughter was born in 2002. We began attending a local church in Plano, Texas, and loved it there, eventually serving the church as Deacon and Deaconess.

Around 2004 strange things began to happen in our home. As time passed, more and more peculiar events started to occur. The first I can remember was feeling extremely uneasy going upstairs; there were two vacant rooms and a landing area up there. I forced myself to go sit upstairs and pray, with the belief that God would stop any act of contention, malice, and harm. Things began to get worse. Amongst several other experiences, our children's bodies had eventually been scratched. Our panicked son used to yell out to me, "Mom, something hit me in the back!" or exclaim, "Something really is in my closet!" I would run to him in the middle of the night while frantically decreeing and declaring the Word of God.

When I prayed to the Lord about him and the situation, I would feel a gentle sweep of wind making an exit toward the door. Our daughter also remembers these encounters. She remembers me going to her room and swaying her in the rocking chair, as I would sing spiritual hymns to her every night. One night after worshiping the Lord in our daughter's room, I smelled a putrid stench that soon went away. The next day, my daughter's school called me and said, "Your daughter is very calm and relaxed today and just wants to sleep." Incidents like these strengthened my faith. I remember thinking, "for I am confident of this very thing, that he who began a good work in me will perfect it until the day of Christ Jesus." (Philippians 1:6 NASB)

Many times, my husband and I felt as if we were suffocating from obstruction during the night. Music that I played on the radio would scratch, then slow down; noises would manifest in other rooms. This force attempted to destroy our family through fear, threat of physical death, and isolation. Isolation? Yes. Reaching out to a few people confused the experience. I felt as though, some mental health professionals chalked my experience up as psychosis or a 'break in reality.' If I was suffering from psychosis, then all four of our family members suffered from this condition. Were all four of us delusional and experiencing hallucinations? On a side note, the cats must have been experiencing psychosis, too, as their heads would whip around looking for a person who was not there. Were there disruptions in the way that I though and perceived my environment? Yes, but it was not difficult for me to recognize what was real and what wasn't. I saw and heard things that other people in the house saw and heard. I was not deranged but experienced depression, weariness, and fear during the battle. In the church, some leadership looked down on what we endured. Some pastors stayed clear. Some would say, "That would never happen to me." What I wanted was support, prayer, and most importantly, deliverance. I eventually believed there was no purpose in reaching out to anyone. I felt mocked, ridiculed, and spiritually put out, so I stopped seeking external support. I do not believe that people were purposely trying to hurt us, as there were several other ministers who were effective in prayer concerning the four of us. I do believe that feeling rejected triggered deeply embedded memories of childhood trauma. Depression and fear continued to rear their ugly heads in what I called "a fiery furnace" – the burning heat was up, but just like Jesus was in the fiery furnace with Shadrach, Meshach, and Abednego (Daniel 3:25 NLT), I knew Jesus was in the furnace with us. We would come out too!

I continued to pray the Word of God, and worship with all that was within me; I knew that if I did not, the stench of torment would persist. Poltergeist made it clear that its intent was death – of our marriage and of our innocent children's reality of almighty God – through depression and fear. Through the comfort of the Holy Spirit, I was able to continue turning my mind towards Jesus. I stood on the scripture, "you will keep him in perfect peace, Whose mind is stayed on You, Because he trusts in You." (Isaiah 26:3 NKJV). I meditated on this scripture too, "For I know the plans I have for you, "declares the Lord," plans to prosper you and not to harm you, plans to give you a hope and a future."(Jeremiah 29:11 NIV). I knew deliverance was going to come. Still, my emotions made it hard to help my loving husband, but he and I stuck together like glue. My husband would rebuke any negative remarks about our marriage – replacing skepticism, ill wishes, and mental brakes with the phrase, "you are a blessed woman"; he never said a word that made me doubt deliverance. Whenever I was depressed, with my head buried under the blankets, my husband would ask, "Is there anything that I can do for you?" If I felt down, he would cook, clean, and take care of the kids. He often said, "We are an incredible team." He was unmovable which allowed me, in time, to truly take hold of the revelation; "...for he who is in you is greater than he who is in the world." (1 John 4:4 ESV), and "But he was wounded for our transgressions, he was bruised for our iniquities: the chastisement of our peace was upon him; and by His stripes we are healed ."(Isaiah 53:5 KJV).

In the following days, I was introduced to Pastor Cindy Trimm's great work, a book titled, The Rules of Engagement: The Art of Strategic Prayer and Spiritual Warfare. I loved how, while praying, she left no spiritual stone unturned; she understood our battle. I began to read her book more than once per day. I played her CD in my car on loop. Cindy Trimm was the one God chose to war with me. Through prayer, she taught me how to call out the lies of anything, and anybody, and the lies that I told myself that would try to suppress deliverance. I began to fist fight in the spirit like I had previously fought in the natural. The discernment of spirit that I used in error to protect myself in a worldly manner was now used to discern when to pray, how to pray, and what to pray. The sword of the Spirit, the Word of God, continued to address the conflict. Every day I continued to worship, read the Word, decree freedom, and cover us, as well as the house, with oil. The Holy Spirit also led me to a local praise and worship dance team where I could minister unto the Lord. My intentions were to worship our way out of this tumultuous situation. As time went on, I began to think to myself, "A few years have passed, why are we still being attacked? Why didn't Poltergeist leave?" Layer by layer, God began to reveal that I was warring from fear – much like how I used to in my early childhood, when I would jump fences while running from danger; or when I would physically find a stick, bat or anything within reach and start swinging when my back was pushed up against a wall – yet, after swinging, I was still afraid. Whatever it took to avoid being subdued or degraded, I did. I would fight from a place of fear and then run for my life like Forest Gump. After all, that's what mom told me to do. She said to "beat 'em, then get out of there." This approach saved my life many times, but this time was different. The Holy Spirit came to me, ministering as clear as day, "Stop running. Stand flat footed for your marriage plus your children and war." Did I not say, for He who is in you is greater than he who is in the world" (1 John4:4 ESV)?

Shortly after, the day of reckoning finally came. My husband went away for the weekend, and the children had been sleeping soundly for a few hours. Then it happened; the night that we would win this battle was here. The most eerie feeling came upon me – almost as if an invisible killer was standing in front of me. It was so intense that my eyes began to water. I had finally decided to stand my ground with no fear. I stood on the verse that I had rememorized early on: O death, where is your victory? "O Death, where is your sting? O Hades, where is your victory?" The sting of death is sin, and the strength of sin is the law. But thanks be to God, who gives us the victory through our Lord Jesus Christ." (1 Corinthians 15: 55 - 57 NKJV).

With conviction, I began to speak every warfare and healing prayer that I had rememorized over the years of my life. The Holy Spirit prompted me to say things that I did not know I knew; I was no longer operating from defense. I declared that this is the Lord's house. I know the truth and the truth has set our family free. My husband and I are free. I think that I even said, "The cats are free." My mouth began to curl upwards with conviction. After several hours of this, I turned around, walked into our bedroom, and laid down without a blanket over my head before going to sleep. Today I laugh whenever I think about that time, because my lips were still like that when I woke up. The next morning was peaceful beyond measure. As I prayed and worshiped Jesus for never leaving or forsaking us, I kept hearing the sweet Holy Spirit say to me, "This will never happen to your family again." I wept like a baby as I heard more. I heard; "I prepared a table before you in the presence of your enemies. I anoint your head with oil; your cup runs over." (Psalm 23:5 KJV).

Yes! The Devil is a liar and there is no truth in him (John 8:44 NIV)!

"There is therefore now no condemnation to them which are in Christ Jesus ..." (Romans 8:1 KJV)! It has been 12 years since that dark time and I still praise Jesus. From what has occurred, our love is now stronger – as well as our marriage; we are two decades strong.

With this triumph came a revelation of what it means to be a Wife Who Wars and a Mother Who Wars. Yes, I am smiling, because I grasped a breathtaking view of Christ's love for us. I take pleasure in visualizing me hanging our wedding picture on a wall along with all the other pictures of marriages that no man or spirit can put asunder. The fiery flames meant to destroy our marriage, have destroyed many strongholds instead. God quenched the fury of our flames and allowed us to escape the edge of the sword. He turned our weaknesses and frustration with time into strength. There is beauty in knowing that we did not give up on God. I smile thinking about how God gave us "beauty for ashes, the oil of joy for mourning, the garment of praise for the spirit of heaviness;" (Isaiah 61:3 KJV). To have the opportunity to share with you how the Holy Spirt exhorted us to draw our swords by reading and being doers of the Word is an amazing feeling. My prayer is that this testimony will encourage you to cling to God for every piece of your marriage. It may sound impossible that fear, heartache, sorrow, condemnation, and mental pain can ever give way to joy. Yet, as an overcomer, I am here to tell you firsthand that, "For his anger lasts only a moment, but his favor lasts a lifetime; weeping my stay for a night, but rejoicing comes in the morning." (Psalm 30:5 NIV). God hears every one of our prayers. God hears our voices in the wilderness. Not one of our tears will fall to the ground unnoticed. No matter what you or your marriage has gone through, whether it be noticed or unnoticed by others, not one moment has escaped the attention of the God who neither slumbers, nor sleeps (Psalm 121:4 NIV).

Grace To Stand!

Mary Jones – Lofton

"Wherefore take unto you the whole armour of God, that ye may be able to withstand in the evil day, and having done all, to stand. Stand therefore, having your loins girt about with truth, and having on the breastplate of righteousness;"
Ephesians 6:13-14 (KJV)

It's going on 35 years and I tell you, there have been some highs and lows. I've always wanted to have a family and get married. I even kept a "hope chest" as a teenager. I laugh at that now because I really didn't realize marriage would have so many challenges.

I got pregnant with our oldest son in my second year of college and when my then boyfriend returned home from the military and asked me to marry him, I thought yes, this is the right thing to do. I was marrying my high school sweetheart.

It's been a journey that has taught me that love is a decision. We were young when we married. I didn't realize how much growth we both needed. I have always been a praying woman, but as time would go on and I grew spiritually, I found out spiritual warfare is not only real, it is necessary for the journey that was ahead of me. Things happen for a reason. They really do! While living in California, the struggle of my husband's addiction began and was short lived with the power of prayer. I grew up understanding the power in prayer but after reading the book, "The Believers Authority," by Kenneth Hagin, Sr., my understanding of prayer changed instantly. I began to understand the scripture Ephesians 6:12 (KJV). "For we wrestle not against flesh and blood, but against principalities, against powers, against the rulers of the darkness of this world, against spiritual wickedness in high places."

My husband re-enlisted into the military and we were stationed in Fort Ord, California. Life was bliss. We relocated to Texas and after several years, what I thought was over changed into a journey that would change me on levels that I couldn't imagine. I quickly learned that this journey was going to be a real, real gut-wrenching daily walk and an infinite lesson to trust in God. My husband's addiction shook me to the core. I realized very quickly that calling folks and telling them what was going on doesn't always help the situation or me. Sometimes people can leave you feeling confused, discouraged, and hopeless. I had a few friends that encouraged me but soon realized it was better to talk to God.

There were times I didn't need a spiritual answer and I tell you, God always gave me what I needed. I had some friends I would call, and they would pray and speak life to me. Elder Sebrina is what I call a bulldog in the spirit. I couldn't call her discouraged. I can laugh now but not at the time. She would say, "Have you read your Word today? Okay, so here is a passage I need you to read and then call me back." When God places a prayer partner in your life, it is a life line. But there were times friends were not available, so I had to depend on God. I was also involved in the Intercessory Prayer Ministry at my church, which God used to keep me focused on who He was in the midst of my life.

Things took a drastic turn when my husband started a job that required him to be out of state for weeks at a time. When home, he would sit in the garage and drink all day and then come inside and argue about any and everything. He became an angry drunk. He would leave the house and would often not return until early the next morning and then want to touch me and act like he did nothing wrong. I would violently push him away. It literally made me want to fight and I'm not talking about in the spirit. I would withhold sex. I did not want to smell the liquor, nor did I want him to feel like he could just act any kind of way and expect me to carry on like all was good. All was not good! I was so relieved when he finally went to sleep. It became harder and harder to see him like that or to even want to be around him. It was hard to pray consistently. I would pray and put the situation in God's hands and take it right back. I would start feeling condemned and unworthy to go back to God in prayer, which I knew was a trick of the enemy and felt lost in that cycle. This went on for almost a year!

One night after my husband left out of state for work, I woke up early in the morning and began to worship and cry out to God.

I was tired of this cycle, I was tired of being tired and needed peace. That morning I experienced God's presence in such a way that I felt a peace and reassurance like never before. The Holy Spirit spoke to me that I was not alone! Hebrews 13: 5-6 (KJV) "Let your conversation be without covetousness; and be content with such things as ye have: for he hath said, I will never leave thee, nor forsake thee. So that we may boldly say, The Lord is my helper, and I will not fear what man shall do unto me." The amplified version says, "neither will I relax my hold on you." That scripture continues to speak to me and gives me the confidence that God has me! From that point, my perspective changed. God would show me over and over that He is God and that no matter what I see with my natural eye, my prayers were impactful. I got my focus back!

I became consistent in prayer! The enemy would still attack my thoughts at times, but I would encourage myself. I would get into worship and speak the Word out loud until what I was declaring drove out the voice of the enemy. I often drove to the park just to have a quiet atmosphere with no distractions to pray. I read several books that ministered to me, The Power of a Praying Wife, by Stormie Omartian, The Battlefield of the Mind, by Joyce Meyers, and Nothing Just Happens, by T. D. Jakes, just to name a few. It is something about being in an atmosphere of nature that helps me become quiet from within and really hear God's voice. I would often visit the Prayer Mountain in Dallas, Texas, on a Saturday morning or right after church on a Sunday. I loved this place. You could just walk and pray out loud and no one would look at you strange. I remember getting there early one Saturday morning and stood out and was just praying in the spirit and a group of African women of God began to join me. Wow, they took it to a whole different level. They prayed with such power. Some of the scriptures I declare over myself to silence the voice of doubt for me:

Psalm 5:11-12 (KJV) "But let all those that put their trust in thee rejoice: let them ever shout for joy, because thou defendest them: let them also that love thy name be joyful in thee. For thou, LORD, wilt bless the righteous; with favour wilt thou compass him as with a shield."

Psalm 91:1-7 (KJV) "He that dwelleth in the secret place of the most High shall abide under the shadow of the Almighty. I will say of the LORD, He is my refuge and my fortress: my God; in him will I trust. Surely he shall deliver thee from the snare of the fowler, and from the noisome pestilence. He shall cover thee with his feathers, and under his wings shalt thou trust: his truth shall be thy shield and buckler. Thou shalt not be afraid for the terror by night; nor for the arrow that flieth by day; Nor for the pestilence that walketh in darkness; nor for the destruction that wasteth at noonday. A thousand shall fall at thy side, and ten thousand at thy right hand; but it shall not come nigh thee."

Psalm 22:5 (KJV) "They cried unto thee, and were delivered: they trusted in thee, and were not confounded."

Numbers 23:19 (KJV) "God is not a man, that he should lie; neither the son of man, that he should repent: hath he said, and shall he not do it? or hath he spoken, and shall he not make it good?"

Proverbs 12:7 (KJV) "The wicked are overthrown, and are not: but the house of the righteous shall stand."

Romans 8:28 (KJV) "And we know that all things work together for good to them that love God, to them who are the called according to his purpose."
Isaiah 32:18 (KJV) "And my people shall dwell in a peaceable habitation, and in sure dwellings, and in quiet resting places;"

Jeremiah 29:11 (KJV) "For I know the thoughts that I think toward you, saith the LORD, thoughts of peace, and not of evil, to give you an expected end."

Isaiah 54:17 (KJV) "No weapon that is formed against thee shall prosper; and every tongue that shall rise against thee in judgment thou shalt condemn. This is the heritage of the servants of the LORD, and their righteousness is of me, saith the LORD."

It helps to declare the scriptures out loud, especially if you are feeling discouraged. It has worked for me and continues to work for me. In addition to my husband working out of state, he had a seizure on the job, which was later diagnosed as withdrawal seizures. Needless to say, with the type of work he did, having seizures caused a safety concern, so they released him. He was now back at home. The seizures continued as he would drink and then abruptly stop. This was heart wrenching to watch him go through this and extremely frightening. He was in denial that the drinking was related to the seizures or that he had a problem. For so long, he would drink and stop for days without any problem. But after a couple of these episodes, he told me he was going to check himself into a program. He finally accepted the fact that his drinking was out of control. This was music to my ears! I watched my husband change into a humble man that was no longer angry.

During my husband's first rehabilitation program, I joined him in several counseling sessions. The counselor began to describe my husband's behavior to the tee and spoke about how addiction causes behavior that has nothing to do with anybody else. Whatever the addiction is, the addictive behavior will display selfishness and blame. My aha moment came as I realized his struggle was a disease and that choices and decisions were only part of the recovery process. Most importantly my husband's addiction is not my fault!

His sobriety would last for a short time and he would go back to the same behavior. I was very disappointed and tried to encourage him to get back into the program. I tried to say everything I could to convince him to return or that he had a problem. I even thought maybe I'm not being harsh enough. Criticizing him and degrading him was not a great motivator. Needless to say, he did not respond to that very well at all. Words are so powerful. I was speaking death into the situation not life. This went on for a while before the revelation came to change what I was speaking. Instead of saying you are stupid if you don't take advantage of rehab, I would say it's a blessing the military will pay for this because many people don't have that option. My heart began to change with a heart of compassion, determination, and a willingness to love my husband no matter what. I wanted to fix my husband's problem, but in the process, God was fixing me. Looking back on things, I would have changed what I was confessing out of my mouth a lot sooner than I did. It didn't matter that I had good intentions, negative words opened the door to the enemy.

I decided not to allow my situation to rule my life. Believe me, I had plenty of opportunities to fly off the handle and get angry. I was working and in school pursuing my degree and was adamant about accomplishing my goals. While at work, I would listen to podcasts and replay the service from that previous Sunday to stay encouraged. I would strongly advise you to be intentional about pursuing peace and not allowing your circumstance to dominate you. Isaiah 26:3 (KJV) "Thou wilt keep him in perfect peace, whose mind is stayed on thee: because he trusteth in thee."

* * *Now when God gives you that crazy peace, it truly is the peace that surpasses all your understanding! I can remember a time I thought, "You know what? I really don't care anymore. I love my husband, but I don't want this anymore." I prayed and told the Lord to just direct me, because I believe it's time to let this marriage go. That was not it at all. God had given me what I had been seeking, Peace! He had strengthened me and had given me another level of grace to stand! I got to the point that all I desired was for God's Will to be done in my life. My husband began to take disrespect to a whole different level! He had questionable female "friends" calling his phone. In prayer, I had specifically asked

God if separating from my husband would help my situation and to give me confirmation. I don't believe in divorce, but I knew others that separated, and it strengthened their marriage. But what is important to remember is everybody's story is not yours.

This particular Sunday while attending The Potters House of Dallas, my Pastor T.D. Jakes was ministering an anointed message and said God says, women you have every reason to leave, but God is saying don't move, but stay. It spoke right into my spirit and I knew I got a Rhema Word! Do you ever get a knowing down in your spirit, and you know that God is speaking to you! I was beyond excited! In my excitement, I shared what happened with a friend. I received the surprising response of "Girl just pray because I think you need to leave. You know Bishop has had messages about not being a doormat." Can you imagine? Here I am excited about what I knew God spoke to me and this was the response.

Basically, the response was telling me that I got it wrong and that the Word was not for me. We have to stay connected to the spirit of God and not people because people will have you living outside of the Will of God. I continued to stand for my marriage. I prayed against those soul ties and saw them totally destroyed.

Then one day I received an invite from my cousin, Denise, to join Wives Who War. God is so strategic. He knew joining this group would be a blessing and that I would gain a lifeline of prayer partners who would deposit pearls of wisdom into my spirit weekly. God provided a Word of encouragement and direction. When I first heard my cousin pray, I knew this was God. She had that bulldog anointing. Being connected to anointed prayer destroys yokes! God knew the days I was discouraged and would use Denise to reach out to me and say, "Mary, I need you to be one of the prayer warriors tonight." As I would pray and declare God's Word, I went from not just believing but to knowing! I continued to pray and always came back to the reminder that this is Spiritual Warfare.

Spiritual Warfare embarks a constant and consistent walk, whether you feel like it or not. Hearing other women of God share their stories helped me see more and more that I was not in this fight alone. I've learned about the power of forgiveness and releasing the bitterness that I thought was gone. I also had an epiphany that no matter how saved you are, trouble hits everyone! Furthermore, seemingly out of nowhere I was laid off my job! I was without work for a total of seven months. I didn't understand why this was happening. This was a total disruption to me and on top of that, my husband would continue to have moments of drowning himself in alcohol, as well as keeping company with unhealthy relationships that fed his addiction that were both male and female, but through it all, I continued to trust God. I would apply for jobs that I was well qualified for and no doors would open. God continued to make provision, but our savings ran out and I was about to receive my last unemployment check. But God! The door He opened was an uncomfortable one. It required relocation. When I went to my husband, he was in agreement to move but was reluctant to sell our home of 25 years. I was surprised that he said he was ready to move and that it would be good to get away from the negative environment he was hanging around. It was going to really require faith because first of all, we didn't have the credit we had before to purchase a new home. I thought okay God, I know you are up to something, but selling our home is a bit much. We relocated, and it was quick. Our home sold the very next month! We settled in and exactly a year later, we bought a new house. It became evident that God strategically moved us.

As I live this journey and see my husband's recovery process continue, I've seen that through every rehabilitation experience, he walks away with something he didn't have before. A burning desire to be totally free! My husband takes each day at a time to walk in his sobriety. Though he has some days of defeat, I rejoice knowing there will be total victory! I continue to believe and stand knowing that God will be glorified and restoration and wholeness is nigh.

Addiction is a stronghold that the power of prayer can and will break. God has proven over and over again that He is yet present. I continue to see God's hand in our lives as I see deliverance unfold. Ironically, our new home backs up to a greenbelt. I am surrounded by a peaceful atmosphere where I can see the beauty of trees and watch the deer in the morning as they graze in the grass. You can't tell me that God is not strategic.

Advice I would give:

- Read a resourceful book all the time. It will help remind you of who God is in the midst of your situation.

- Pray and confess God's Word, even when you don't feel like it. This is a faith move and God will honor it.

- Ask God to send you a prayer partner. There is power in agreement.

- Find a place of peace when you are having a tough day or just want to get your spirit quiet and get you back in focus. God will meet you there!

The Devil Didn't Win

Jean Burns

"And now these three remain: faith, hope and love. But the greatest of these is love."

1 Corinthians 13:13

Saturday, February 24, 2007 will be a day that tremendously changed my family's life.

Waiting seemed forever when a team of doctors tells you that your spouse must have emergency surgery on his back to fix a minor pinched nerve. I waited for hours, rubbing my nine-month-old belly, happy that I continued to feel my baby kicking because of stress. After about ten hours of patiently waiting, my husband was wheeled into the room, still asleep. I noticed that the nurses had minimal conversation and eye contact with me after I repeatedly asked how his surgery went.

Three more hours went by, then a team of ten doctors appeared, looking concerned and speaking in medical terminology that was foreign to me. One doctor took a scalpel in his hand, which he forced into the middle part of my spouses' foot, to test his reflex. My husband was without a flinch or a reaction. I knew something went wrong. When I saw the blood dripping down his foot onto the bed, I jumped to my feet and ask what was going on? I suddenly started to feel very dizzy, I could no longer hear what the doctors were trying to convey to me.

When I finally came to, the team of doctors were still looking at my husband with concern, who was now awake with a look of despair on his face. I was trying to regain my focus; one doctor started moving towards me as if he needed me to hear and understand what he was saying. He then said, "Ma'am, your husband has experienced a stroke during surgery which severed his spine, leaving him paralyzed." I stood up and walked out of the hospital, never to return to visit my spouse for two months.

I gave birth February 27 to a beautiful seven-pound baby boy. I was young, confused, and depressed from previous situations that had transpired. I had three nervous breakdowns over a short period of time and wondered if I was mentally stable to raise three healthy children while taking care of a newly paralyzed spouse. I was overwhelmed with depression and my mother stepped in to take care of my two oldest children, ages four and five, to live with her. My mom realized how unstable I was mentally and wanted to minimize my daily load. She left the newborn because I was breastfeeding him, but I knew the pain that I was enduring was unbearable, and I should have sent him away as well. I realized I was battling more than hurt. I was fighting personal and impersonal feelings. I started drinking, not quite an alcoholic but not far from it. I stayed up most nights crying, drinking, and not responding to my newborn as he cried himself to sleep from lack of attention. I was in denial about severely suffering from postpartum depression. I couldn't come to grips that I was in shock, I walked out on my spouse in the hospital, I did not have two of my children, and I was alone. I had heard from my mom that they moved my husband from the hospital to a rehabilitation center to teach him how to regain the use of his new body, but I was still going through depression. I stayed up the night before thinking, feeling very emotional, frustrated, and conflicted. I asked myself could I be an obedient, loving, caring wife to my spouse for better or worse, through sickness and health, till death do us part and still raise three mentally stable and loving children? One morning while in the bathroom, a powerful entity accompanied me. Their presence was so vigorous, my thoughts moved me to the mirror to look at myself. As I leered at myself, I was in disbelief of how far I had fallen into depression as I looked at myself. I heard a distinctive voice say to me, pray! Pray like your soul depends on your allowing God to come in your life and restore you. Pray for your existence, pray for discernment, pray for coherence, pray anyway necessary and I will hear you. I began to speak, feeling that nothing I said would matter. I fell to my knees right where I stood becoming immovable. I cried out, "Lord, I need you. I need you, Lord. I need you to restore me to make me whole again. I know I can't do this without you. Lord, I tried, and I know now it is impossible. I need help!" The dominant presence said, "Get up, clean your house, cleanse your soul, and nourish your body." At that very moment, I regained my strength to move and become stable on my feet. I immediately took a shower and washed off yesterday's burdens to lighten my load. I prayed and asked God for forgiveness for doubting Him because I was lost within myself. I poured out my toxic situation into the drain and began to think and process things rationally.

God gave me the strength to bond with my newborn child. I was able to shower him with an abundance of love. God also gave me the strength to drive to pick up my two oldest children from my mom's house and take them home. I had been absent from my children's lives for months, and I knew they were worried and wanted to see me. Most importantly, God gave me the strength to make my way to see my husband after two months of being absent from his life in his time of need. Unaware to him, I had come to visit and was watching him struggle to balance on his bottom. As he fell over, our eyes locked, I saw disappointment and gratitude in his eye all at the same time. We both teared up, and we shared an overwhelming emotional cry that should have taken place when we were first told he would never walk again. I held him tight, expressing myself and telling my story with my touch and the compassion I carried in my eyes. I was apologetic and very watchful of every word that came out of my heart.

I stopped periodically to pray and ask God for direction when I felt myself becoming frustrated or impatient with different situations stemming from my spouse's new life change. My husband struggled with acceptance of not being able to be the strong man for our family that God directed him to be. I relied on God often when I couldn't speak. I spoke to Him in my thoughts, I just laid there, confident that he would restore in me what I continued to struggle with, "adapting."

My husband stayed in the rehabilitation center for a year and a half, allowing his body and mind, to replenish, reconstruct and adapt. He was ready to be discharged when the doctors told him he was unable to return home because gangrene had set into both legs and he was very ill. I stayed by his side day and night as he tried to fight off a 103 degrees temperature. I called one person, my youngest sister, and I remember telling her I couldn't continue to stress alone. Right before my eyes, she had sent a team of prayer warriors to the hospital to praise our awesome God. They surrounded my husband's bedside with prayers, laughter, singing and allowed me to be vulnerable during that situation. That night, my spouse's fever went down, and he was cleared for surgery. I knew God was on our side. He showed up, showed out and made our unit even tighter. I prayed to God, and I asked him to take control of my husband's surgery and allow him to come back to our family. He returned as a double amputee with one above the knee and one below the knee amputation. He was very emotional but doing great. After four days, I returned home to my young children, tired not stressed; I was relieved.

Life has continued to put many obstacles and distractions at the forefront of our lives. April 2009, my husband was doing physical therapy when he became dizzy, telling his trainer that he had developed a blood clot in his left leg and he immediately needed to be taken to the hospital. After being taken to the hospital and admitted, he was told he had developed one blood clot in his left leg and two clots in his lungs. That night I was told that my husband would probably suffer a heart attack and pass away. I was a firm believer that God had other plans, but I respectfully called his family just in case that was His plan. His family and friends came to wish him well. Not one person prayed. I had enough. I asked his family and friends to go home and let him rest. That night I only thanked God for coming into our lives and redirecting us to Him. I thanked God for giving me an abundance of strength to continue to take care of my family. I thanked God for all the time I was allowed with my spouse, and I gave all my worries and doubt to Him. As I watched my husband sleep, my eyes became heavy. The next morning both myself and my husband woke up staring at one another. I knew at that very moment we both gave God a silent prayer to thank him for never leaving our side. God sends His hedge of protection to surround our family with strength and guidance. He only asks of us to trust His process.

He arrived home differently this time from the hospital. My husband had been paralyzed for eight years now. He never accepted professional help with coping with becoming paralyzed and losing the use of his manhood. He was frustrated, bed bound and exempt from the world that continued to proceed without him. My spouse never interacted with the outside world for years. He suffered mentally finding an outlet in arguing and accusing people out from situations that were not happening. He started to indulge in YouTube videos, watching people discuss the world ending, which made him overly prepare for the world catastrophes. How do you tell someone you love that they are suffering from mental deprivation? I didn't, and his life drained the soul out of my life.

I was in my early thirties; I had a lot of evolving to accomplish. I had conditioned myself to believe I was happy because I was financially stable. I was sexually frustrated; I was mentally tired of being accused of many things that I was not doing. God showed me self-love and He gave me permission to have my voice back. I went for so long afraid to speak my truth, nervous to hurt someone's feeling and content with the lifestyle that was given to me. I wanted to live but was trapped in someone else's life. God showed me that He could give it, and He can take it away.

I manifest that we have an awesome God that loves all His children. I rely on God to devise decisions for my family and me. I have always needed God; I depend on Him more now than I ever have in life. The cultivation of my being a great wife and mother allowed me to become a diligent child of God. I stayed on my knees in prayer and I wasn't afraid to ask for help, nor forgiveness because I knew my Heavenly Father never has forsaken me.

12 years have passed, and my spouse and I are stable in our walk with God as individuals but not as a whole. We both have become comfortable with lack of communication and togetherness. My husband struggles with interaction with family and friends. He also struggles with coping, afraid that his new life will separate him from society and put him in a box filled with disabled people that cannot function in a world with ordinary walking people. He struggles to love, communicate, and adapt to his life after 12 years of being paralyzed — the children suffer from lack of affection from their dad, which led me to put them into counseling. I pray with them and direct them back to God when they are feeling overwhelmed. Our kids struggle to connect to their father, whose attention is on staying healthy and not necessary parenting. They're much older and can interpret their dad's actions into their own words. No matter the situation, God is always giving me the tools

to continue to keep my family connected to him and balanced.

In conclusion, marriage is a balance. You have to put God first. You have to communicate and understand that marriage is work. Two people are joined together to become one, and both are trying to hang onto their independence, their voice to remain heard.

One may not be ready to allow the other to lead, and one may not be leading correctly. Marriage is most definitely a compromise. Both parties have to know his or her position when balancing a successful marriage. If you continue putting God first and focus on yourself and not what he/she are doing or not doing, you will have a better outcome dealing with situations in your marriage. "God first. Everything else second."

We have spoken about divorce more times than I would like to mention. The love is lost, and each partner expects more from the other partner but not willing to do the work anymore. More lately,

I am living by "WWJD." ("What Would Jesus Do?") When I find myself in situations I cannot wiggle out of, I ask myself what would Jesus do and guide myself back into having a healthy balanced life. Remember, if you always call on the Lord, He will come into your life and never leave, even when you feel He has. By the time this book comes out, I know without a shadow of a doubt, I will be divorced. My spouse continues to ignore me, he is not appreciative of the things I effectuate, and he has started to be physically and mentally abusive to me. I left for myself. Along the way, I developed self-love. I put myself and my kids first. We had suffered enough and from now on we want to LIVE!

"When my heart is overwhelmed Lead Me To The Rock That Is Higher Than I" Psalm 61:2. Ten questions I ask myself as a guide in my marriage:

1. Are you putting God first?
2. Are you praying and asking for guidance?
3. Are you making the commitment it takes to have a successful marriage?

4. Are you surrounded by positive prayer warriors that will direct you and your spouse back to your leader?

5. Are you focused on yourself and what you need to improve?

6. Do you have self-love?

7. Do you know how to convey in words what you need?

8. Do you communicate well?

9. Do you approach situations with God's guidance?

10. Do you feel lost in your marriage?

Seeing It Through To Completion

Pastor Cynthia Jackson

"Nevertheless, that time of darkness and despair will not go on forever."

Isaiah 9:1

My story is current and still being written. There are many that often ask the question, "How did you two make it this long? You seem to be so in love." or "You could not have been married that long, Pastor!!!" The response is, "Jesus." We never could have made it without Jesus. There are times that the response is, "You see this time and place? You are not viewing what it took to arrive here." The question is well understood today because marriages barely make it two years now; so even though it is hard to believe, we are now in our 43rd year.

Our marriage has weathered many storms and made it to shore safely without being consumed by the sea. There may have been times that we made it to shore on the plank, but I assure you it was God showing us that He just needs a remnant, and He will use it for His glory. I truly wish that I could tell you that I've seen it all, however, that would be arrogant and a setup for the enemy to wage an attack and show me that I really have not. What I can say is that this marriage covenant has seen a lot and I'm wise enough to say that if Jesus does not return, we will see more. The treasure that I will share with you is that as you read, know that I still hold onto the fact that as long as Jesus is front and center, we can get through whatever life throws our way. There are times that truly we may not want to continue on, but that is when the Holy Spirit that lives inside of us will remind us that we can't do it, but if we will allow Him to work through us, we can make it. The operative word is "Will we allow Him or Are we willing?"

My husband and I met while I was on vacation visiting my sister in San Francisco. It was a beautiful Sunday morning, and we did what our family does, we went to church. My niece introduced us standing outside church and we talked a little bit. He inquired how long I would be in town. He let me know he was home from college and would love to take me sightseeing in the City. He picked me up in his two-toned green Pontiac Firebird and took me on the first of many dates to see the great sights in San

Francisco. He did not miss a day coming by to pick me up and take me somewhere different. We were starting a friendship. We laughed a lot, and he was quite a gentleman. He was out to impress me, and he did. This proved to be a wonderful summer for the two of us, but each of us had to return to our reality and the other relationships that we were in.

We would continue to communicate with each other. In 1973/74, we did not have cell phones, so we wrote a lot of letters and made a few phone calls. We would be happy to hear each other's voice, but the mailbox was our friend. This long-distance friendship would prove to be the foundation for what was to come many years later. He sent me gifts through the mail. Wayne drove across country to Chicago for the first time, the summer of 1975, and spent a couple of weeks staying at my eldest brother's home.

A two-year long-distance relationship with college and obligations let us know that we wanted to be in closer proximity to each other. I wasn't finding the University of Illinois the place that I wanted to be at that time. My mother, known as MaDear, made it real clear to me. She said, "When you finished high school, that was for me. What you do after that is for your life. You get to make that decision." Wayne purchased me a plane ticket and asked me if I'd accept it and move to California. He even did the groundwork to determine where I was going to live. His grandfather had a small apartment in his building if I needed it, or he talked with my brother-in-love (he is my second Dad since he has been a part of my life before I was 2 years old), and while he would have preferred I finish college, he talked with my sister and let her know it was okay for me to move-in. He has often told me he did not regret his decision. October 1975 the move occurred, and I was in San Francisco to stay. I secured a job within two weeks and never looked back. Wayne had made a decision to give up his college football career. What I can say is that as young adults, love, or what you think is love, will make you do things that you can look back and say if someone of wisdom had spoken truth and told me that true love will be there when you complete your degree, it is possible that different decisions would be made.

Wayne proposed to me on Christmas Day 1975. We knew we wanted to spend the rest of our lives together, or so we thought.

We started planning a wedding for June, however, that changed suddenly to Valentine's Day. A friend of ours, who has since passed away, got into a very bad car accident and his life was changed forever. Suddenly time had a different meaning to us. The biggest decision for us was would the wedding be in California or Illinois? We came to an agreement after some wise words were spoken that the bride was being taken from her family and therefore – Chicago it was. The wedding was planned without nine months to a year of stress and could not have been better. We married in the church that was my true foundation with a reception in Chicago and

San Francisco. We were off to a blissful future. Love makes you see things as a fairytale.

It is amazing that our wonderful little one bedroom, one bath apartment that was filled with new furniture was cozy and just right for the two of us in San Fran. We had one car at that time. The bus and streetcars were near, and we had a grocery store in the neighborhood.

Our first three years were spent enjoying ourselves. We had the freedom to come and go as we pleased. Our work schedules were different in the first year. When he came home, I had dinner ready and would sit and have a snack with him as I had been informed by my mother. She gently told me once that it was important that I spend time with him when working different schedules. He later changed jobs and we would meet up after work and go to various events or after work socials. Other times, we entertained in our little apartment, playing dominoes and games with friends. We were social beings, or so it appeared that way as we were always doing something.

In 1977/78, I was scouted by a software company in the Silicon Valley. I accepted the job and commuted from San Francisco to Santa Clara for many months before moving to Santa Clara.

The third year of marriage would take us into new territory, we would be blessed with our first child. We welcomed our first son, Andre. We were now responsible for a little person. If we had known that I was pregnant, we would not have left the city, because we had no family in the valley. Now as we look back, we know God was preparing us to stand strong – nowhere to run. During the pregnancy, I would experience a major accident with my left hand. This was the first medical trial.

Now with the responsibility of a family, my husband would find himself unemployed and us needing to find a new place because the lovely community we lived in was an adult only complex. Our closest family was 50+ miles away. Wayne will

tell you he prayed and let God know he had a family
he needed to care for and God granted him the job
that he would retire from 33 years later. Our regular
routine was to travel to San Francisco for church
each week. That was not a normal occurrence as
commuters grace the highway today. When it was
time to go back to work when Andre was about 6
months old, I had to trust God for daycare. I can tell
you that after making the wrong choice, God directed
us back to the one He had shown us first, Melva.
Melva loved our child and cared for him as her own
with lots of love. 40 years later and retired out of
state, we still keep in touch.

Life was changing. It wasn't as easy to get up
and go now. We had to plan because we needed
babysitters if we were going out. As time moved on,
I would experience life becoming different because
Wayne was able to get off work and have freedom to
go as he desired, and I was not able to. One day I
realized my husband often worked a split shift and
would get home late and Andre would be in the bed

or ready for bed. It was decided he would give the baby breakfast and take him to Melva when he started late. This allowed them to spend more time together building a relationship. I would pick my child up from daycare and run errands or make the park our first stop the summer months so that he and I could play. We would then go home and have dinner or go out to a restaurant.

Now it was my turn - My company would have a major layoff and of all the people they laid off (over 100), I was the only one that they offered a job in another department based on my background. This was the first time I had experienced a layoff and didn't understand the people crying and their lives being devastated. I declined the offer, prepared to enjoy the summer and return to college. I am pleased to say that I did take classes and the company would call me again, and I returned to work for them on my terms and continued going to school. I can tell you that God granted the opportunities. Andre would see me get my AA degree and by 1983, we would become homeowners.

In 1984, we would welcome our second son, Anthone. This pregnancy was difficult, but God saw us through a rare pneumonia, blood clot, and stomach sprain. With the second child, we were still commuting to church in the city. Both of us are singing in the choir and I am in a mission circle. I can tell you that we were both laying a foundation for our children, but really just doing our Jesus time, not truly in relationship with Christ. This is where life begins to change.

In my spirit, I am feeling something is not right. As Wayne is getting dressed and pulls out his suit to go out, I get dressed and he said, "Where you going?" I said, "With you." In my innermost being I can feel something is up, but I can't put my hand on it. I went with him that night, and we barely talked. I sat right there at the bar next to him. Cell phones were not in our possession at that time. I didn't know who she was, but I knew she existed. A woman that is not jealous can trust her inner person because she is not making things up in her mind.

We had been through the struggle of the drugs that had a stronghold. I thought that was tough and wondered how I could make it out of this. We had seen drugs destroy some of our friends, however, what had been recreational was now more than that. I can remember God revealing to me that even though I wasn't playing in this field now, I was an accessory to this. You see, when we were dating and first married and he occasionally smoked a joint, I was okay with it. But one day I said to him, "Stop taking stuff from people. You should buy your own. You don't know what they have bought!!" God showed me clearly the $5 bag was the beginning of freedom and I had to see my part in it.

Some years later I was surprised to discover one day the mortgage was behind. This is when I realized things were not good. As I look back, the pattern was being set long before. Things can be changing, and one is in it and they don't realize it. On the surface, it all looks good. We go to some events together, but we are socializing a lot separately. I can remember sitting the boys down and asking, "if we separate, who do you want to go with?" This was a tough one because as I looked in the eyes of my children, they were being forced to make a choice and, sadly, they were choosing their Mom because as males, they are protective of their mom. The reality is that I know they have a very strong relationship with their Dad and as I heard and I looked at them, my heart hurt. You see, we didn't think we were going to pull out of this one.

This time I was really planning my exit strategy and the big hurdle was to tell MaDear (this was big). You see, my Mom and Dad had a good marriage. They overcame many things and worked them through until death did they part. We didn't know my Dad was a man like any other man because we believed he was next to God. MaDear didn't paint a negative picture and Daddy never let us see it – that was adult business. I never put MaDear in our business, which is what she always told her sons and daughters. We heard her say, "If you don't put other people in your business, you won't have to worry about them looking at you cross eyed when you make up." She only gave advice if asked or if she saw you headed toward devastation.

I remember standing in my kitchen and calling her on the phone to let her know we were going our separate ways – she stopped me and said, "Cynthia, it takes communication. You need to pray." We never discussed it again because I realized later that MaDear simply sought the Lord and called on a couple of more people to come together daily and pray for our marriage. God showed me that later and then confirmed by one of my sisters. They prayed together, not gossiped, for God to intervene and He heard their prayers. I hadn't told any of the women in my Bible study. You see, we met every Monday and went through books that strengthened us in our Christian walk, however, I wasn't about to share this problem with them. I can tell you that God had placed, as He has so many times over the years, an older woman that walked in the office of a prophet (I really didn't understand it then as I do now). She always took me to scripture when God showed her what was going on and she would pray with me. Aunt Mary never talked about my husband, she simply guided me and prayed with me.

When Wayne and I were having a heart to heart, he confessed that there was another woman. I don't remember the pain today, but I remember I cried a river, and he heard the pain in the cry. I had been faithful to him and even though I sensed it, now I knew it. After three days, I called my son's godfather to meet me after work and shared my heart with him. As a man, he had a great deal of respect for Wayne, but I guess he had placed him on a pedestal. He told me his only concern was the drugs that he witnessed for himself. He assured me that day that I did not have to worry about him leaving me for what he called a flip skirt. He said, "Wayne knows that he has a good woman. He is not going to allow a flip skirt to mess that up." At that moment, I wasn't sure; however, I remember leaving there feeling better because I had let that burden go. Suddenly, many of the teachings that I had heard from the older woman would come back to me. The prophet didn't need me to tell her, but began to give me scriptures to read, and prayed with me. I remember saying I just want our marriage to go back the way it was. She was straightforward, letting me know it was not going to be the same, because trust was broken. God was going to put it back together the way He wanted it. I remember making a conscience decision that this was my husband and that no one was going to take him from me, and I was not giving him away. We were building something that was worth continuing. The decision to stay in the marriage required the decision that intimacy is a must. I remember praying and asking God to give me the strength and the desire because it is easy to say "no," but it's harder to say "yes." In fact, I remember him asking me, "Why did you make love to me?" I knew that it was necessary because if not, the distance grows wider. Over the next few weeks, I asked questions about the other relationship. He and I talked and then I had to let it go and realize it was over. The most important understanding was that she was the escape from reality (responsibility, family). He did not allow her to put demands on him. It took a while to stop wondering when he left the house and was gone for a while if he was with her. I finally was able to tell myself, "I will not be hostage to this. I will trust him." This was truly the beginning of learning to war.

As time has advanced, I have learned to trust God when times are good as well as trying. The enemy didn't know when, but he knew God would use us for his service. I answered a call to ministry in 1992. Being in a so-called man's world was not new to me because as I was excelling to the executive row, I was, in reality, in a man's world. This would bring about another obstacle as my husband answered his call a couple of years later. We've had to overcome those in the church comparing our preaching styles and asking who the head is. In this instance, I hold fast to Galatians 3:28 and then let it be known that "My husband is the head of our household" and we get to serve together in ministry. I have learned to not allow outsiders to override what God has stated. In 1998, I was offered an amazing opportunity in Chicago which would result in my commuting for two years. It was in this season that my husband and I both learned what real trust is. I sat down with my sons before starting that journey and let them know that there would be those that would ask if they needed anything and the answer was to be "No," and I gave them the names of the three women that could bring food to the house besides family. That chapter was good, and in 2000, we made a decision that I was coming back to California – I began making plans and starting to pack. Within a couple of days, the company decided to reorganize, God gave me my out.

The move back to California would result in a couple of moves, as well as jobs, eventually giving notice to a secular job to accepting a full-time ministry position. Three years later, God was calling me to leave that staff position to start a church in Manteca.

It has not been an easy road, but it is a road I'm called to travel. I've learned to close my mouth and pray when the wrong words are coming. Together we know to pray before having serious talks. As I'm writing this story, I am warring. My Apostle Sister would say, "I'm under friendly fire." I'm holding to Philippians 1:6 - He shall see it to completion!!!!!

Prayer Has A Hold On Me

Jennifer James-Lewis

"Rejoice always, pray continually, give thanks in all, circumstances for this is God's will for you in Christ Jesus."
1 Thessalonians 5:16, 17, 18 (NIV)

In thinking of marriage, girls imagine what their wedding would be like, their wedding gown, lots of friends and family, etc. What I did not know was what it took to make a marriage work after the wedding. The world concept of marriage is first comes love and then comes marriage. If you fall out of love, just divorce him. But that's not real. I didn't know what it really meant until I got married. I have been married before, and I had the big church wedding and beautiful gown. Being young, I did not know what marriage was really about and what it takes to be in "married." I had my parents as examples and my grandparents who have been married for years. My mother used to tell me, "Pray, and never go to bed angry. Talk out your differences." Wisdom from your parents. Pray about what is going on in your marriage.

I was going to a church that a friend attended, and I started going there also. I got baptized. I was learning about Christ but did not know Christ Jesus. I thought, well, serve God and be faithful in church.

Then I would get married. I met my first husband in my early twenties. I dated him for about a year and a half. He was in the Navy. We got married. I did not know myself, but I knew I did not want to be single all my life. My friends were telling me to wait, but I went on and got married. My husband was from New York and I was from California. He had just gotten out of the Navy and had to find a job. Once he had a job, we saved up some money. My parents helped us get our first place.

I thought that our marriage was going to be just fine, myself going to church. My husband stayed at home. Sometimes he would go, but then he realized that he wanted to follow the Muslim way. He would ask me to follow him at that church. I would say, no my family did not bring me up in following the Muslim way. I told him I would not step foot in that church. He would argue with me about that subject. I would still say no, then problems would arise with his drinking. I would pray about it, like my mother told me and it seemed the problems got worse. He lost his job. I still had my job, but that was not enough. My husband and I were eventually behind on bills. I kept on praying and was wondering why I still had problems. Marriage was not supposed to be this way. I talked it over with my friends and they would say, you were too young to get married.

I went for advice in my church. My pastor, at the time, and his wife would lead me back to the Word of God. Looking at prayer, the scripture that would come to me would be Psalm 23. I would read it and kept on praying. I would have hoped my husband would change. He kept on drinking. Then I found some woman's phone number in his pants pocket. He would deny it. I was very angry and hurt. I did leave him and stayed gone for about a month. I did not know if I wanted to leave the marriage. We decided to work on our marriage. Our marriage was going okay. He still would not go to church, but I kept on praying, never giving up hope.

Then the arguments started again. He stayed gone all night. Never had he stayed gone all night. I found out he was having an affair with another woman. I was worried about him. Then he came home the next morning. I confronted him, asking where he had been all night. We argued and I decided it was enough. I packed my bags and left him. I eventually filed for divorce. I was hurt and angry. My trust in people was not the same. I never imagined that I would end up divorced. I was divorced without any kids. I wanted them, but that isn't what happened. I never gave up on prayer, nor went off the path. My mother confronted me and said to me that I stopped going to church. I did stop going to church. I wanted to do it my way. I didn't want to listen to anyone. But it didn't work. My mother and grandmother were raised in the church. My mother kept on praying for me.

I did eventually go back to church with a friend who invited me to her church. I would go with her, and I got involved in the praise ministry. We became good friends. She introduced me to a young man who was in jail. He gave me his information and

I started to write him. We developed a friendship, and I eventually went to see him. After seeing him several times, one day he asked me to marry him. I had not known him for very long. He had a few more years before being released from jail. He told me that I could marry him in jail. After thinking about it, I thought I'd give marriage another chance.

I knew he read the Bible or, at least, that is what he told me. I decided that I would marry him, then went to the jail and got married. No one knew about this marriage, except a friend of mine. I knew inside of me it was wrong. He was excited that we were finally married. This would have been my second marriage and his first. We were separated because he still had to finish his time. I would go up and see him as often as I could, or he would call me on the phone. Then he talked to me about wanting children.

I wanted children, but he was still in jail. I thought about the decision that I made after going forth with the marriage and knew it was wrong, so I annulled the marriage. When it was done, I was still going through hurt and anger from the first marriage. Then when I married again the second time, I was not healed from the first marriage.

I still had anger issues, but I never gave up. I met a woman who ministered to me about prayer. She would talk to me about prayer and having a relationship with God. She would pray with me and minister to me about God. That is when I started to really have a prayer life. She mentored me for years. I started serving in the church as a single and started to heal from my past hurts. I got my first degree and continued my education, working on myself. Then I got my driver's license. I would fail the test the first time, then one day I passed.

I kept on praying and believing in God. As I kept serving in church, I was getting older, but I knew I wanted to be married. I wanted a marriage that was going to last. I would see more single woman in church than there were men. I would ask God as I was serving in the church, why are there so many single women in the church? It seemed to me my friends were getting married and having children. They looked happy. Why couldn't it be like that for the single woman in the church. Again, I would ask God why are there so many single women in the church? He would refer me back to the Bible. There were some married woman who would tell me to just wait on God, but I would think to myself, you are married. You have a husband at home. It's easy for you to say.

Then I would ask God, what about those women who have been single for years? They are still waiting. Then one day a woman ministered to me and told me that God had a husband for me. She said that God had to do some things in me first. I got excited and felt that I was not forgotten.

Some years went by, I was getting older and still without any children. I was thinking, well, maybe I'll just help God a little bit. That does not work. God does not need our help, and I realize that now. A friend of mine met her husband online on a dating website. She dated him and they got married. I thought if it worked for her, maybe it might work for me. I met my current husband. We have been married for about three years now, going on four years, the longest I have been married. When we were engaged, I remember God saying that I would be on my knees a lot. When I got married, I thought about that but still went on and got married.

Both of us were raised in church. He would tell me about going to church with his grandmother. Even though we went to church, we both still had a lot to learn about marriage. He was retired and stayed at home. My husband opened up to me about the church hurt that he had experienced and shared with me his feelings about it. He expressed to me about the physical hurt in his own life but was still helping out in the ministry. I learned that he was hurting but was covering up his feelings.

It was my husband who would keep the house clean and cook all the meals. He made sure I never wanted for nothing. He still had some issues to deal with. He would drink sometimes and smoke. When I would talk to him about it, he would say that he would stop. I would pray that he would do so. He eventually did stop drinking, but he still smoked. When I would talk to him about the smoking, my husband would brush it off, and said he could stop. There were times we would get into arguments, yelling and screaming. Crying would do no good. When I realized it wasn't doing any good, I thought about when the Holy Spirit told me that I would be praying a lot. That's what I did.

I realized that when you marry, you are as one. No more making decisions on your own. you had to discuss them with your husband. I would pray, spending more time with God. I realized I thought I knew how to be a wife, but I did not. I started to look at scriptures and really read the Bible. I would keep feelings to myself a lot, which didn't help, covering up what I really felt and not being honest with myself or my husband. I was frustrated.

Then one day I was talking to a friend and she told me to never give up on prayer. Keep praying for your husband and God will work that issue out.

Prayer was always brought back to me. When we made decisions concerning the household, we weren't making them together.

He would make the decision. Sometimes I agreed, but when I expressed how I felt and disagreed, the arguments would start. The Holy Spirit revealed to me that when decisions are made in marriage, it is very important that you have unity. It has to be a coming together. The Bible says, Again truly I tell you that if two of you on earth agree about anything they ask for, it will be done. "For where two or three gather in my name, there am I with them". Matthew 18:20 (NIV) There have been times when we came together in prayer and prayed together, that issue would be worked out. It showed me that when husband and wife come together in unity, how God works out the problem.

There was a time when my husband and I were living in a one- bedroom apartment. We got accepted in the first home buyer program. My husband and I were excited. We looked for our home, sometimes having conflicts on the house. I would like it and he would not. We looked in different cities, but nothing would work out or my husband did not like the house. The Holy Spirit revealed to me the house that my husband and I were going to live in was a three-bedroom, two bath home. That is why those other houses wouldn't work out.

My husband was looking at some houses online. He said, "Let's go look at some houses in that city." At first I did not want to go but gave in and went to that city. We looked at several houses, then we found the one in which we currently live. I liked the house the first time I saw it, and it was a three-bedroom, two bath home, just like the Holy Spirit said. We packed up and moved away from the city in which we were living. We settled down in our new home, but I was still working in the Bay Area. I liked my job, but I had to drive two hours to work, and back home. I quit my job, stepped out on faith and looked for a job that was closer to my home. My husband would always take me to my job interviews. He would pray for me to find a job closer to home. During that time our bills were paid, and our mortgage was paid. It was months later that I found a job as a teacher. I continued to work at the company and, eventually, took the job where I am currently employed. I am lead teacher in that classroom. I loved my job, which paid more money working part time. I was happy there.

Then one day my husband said that he did not want to live in the city that we were in. He expressed that he wanted to move back to his state where he was from. I didn't. We argued, and he changed his mind about moving out of state. He expressed we could find a home closer to my job. I loved our home and did not want to move. I prayed and fasted about the decision we were making on our home. During that time, we were doing a lot of arguing about the decision concerning the move. My husband put the house on the market to be sold. I was very upset about the decision. It made no sense to me to move, not having a plan where we were going to live. My mother came to visit. She lived out of state. She loved my home, and said it was beautiful but sensed the arguing that was going on between my husband and me. My mother told me to pray about it and to discuss my feelings with my husband. Prayer was again being told to me. At the time, my husband was praying, and I was praying but not with each other. I know what happens when you pray together in unity and experience how the Holy Spirit works out a situation.

Trust issues began to happen, and I accused him of not being faithful. I would go through his phone, but the Holy Spirit revealed to me that I needed to trust my husband. Past hurts came back that I thought I was delivered from. At the time, my husband and I were both attending the same church. He stopped going. Then we began to argue about that issue. I was going through so much in my marriage, past hurts were coming back up, even while I was in prayer. The Holy Spirit would reveal faith to me, telling me to stop looking at my situation in the natural. I did some self-examination and went into my prayer closet, praying and fasting, crying out toward my marriage and situation regarding our home.

Then the Holy Spirit revealed repentance. When you come to the Holy Spirit, you must come with a pure heart. I was directed to the scripture, Psalm 51:10 (NIV), about coming clean with your sin.

My suggestion would be to keep praying. The Holy Spirit showed me that I would have to trust my husband. I stopped looking in his phone and realized that we were on the same team. When you work together, the Issue can be worked out. I knew that, but we hadn't been praying together. Covering up your feelings is no good. Talking to your husband about what is on your heart is the best way to communicate.

Another suggestion is getting prayer from your church family or counseling. I never had counseling. My friend would talk to me and encourage me, praying with me and her sister, who was also in the church. They would call me, and we would pray together. I started talking to my husband, took off the mask and communicated with him. When you talk to each other and not at one another, issues can be solved. The house was still on the market, but I was given peace about the living situation.

Most important is faith. Stop looking at it in the natural but trust the Holy Spirit to work out the situation. When I stopped worrying about the issues and gave the problems to the Holy Spirit, I started seeing how God was going to work out my living situation. Faith is what moves the Holy Spirit. I leaned on this scripture a lot in prayer: Hebrews 11:1-2 NIV and Proverbs 3:5-6 NIV.

My suggestion is to pray before you get married. Getting advice and talking to people in your church does help or talk to your family. Getting counsel does help the situation. I did not get counseling, but I should have talked to someone. It could have saved me a lot of pain. My husband and I have started talking to one another and praying together. We have a long way to go, but now prayer has come back in our home. The most important is prayer, and never give up. Keep praying. Using faith will get the Holy Spirit moving on your situation. The key thing is to keep on praying and never give up!

The Ties That Bind Are The Ones God Ties

Dr. Karen Amos, D.TH

Looking back in retrospect of the prayers that were made to God, He has never failed to answer or supply. When on prior occasions you have lost in love, raised children as a single parent and past the age of conceiving anymore children, you begin to settle into life identified "as is!"

This is it Lord, I'm satisfied with you and thank you for seeing us through life's every twist and turn. After years of prayers and waiting for the promise of God, in a loving man of God to be a husband, a father, and a co-laborer in Christ in ministry, I had settled into my life and put it on cruise control the rest of the way. There was one thing I neglected to consider, God's timing was not my timing. Jeremiah 29:11 (Berean Study Bible) For I know the plans I have for you, declares the Lord, plans to prosper you and not to harm you, to give you a future and a hope.

God's timing, being quite different from ours, is the Creator of whom set into existence seasons, years, days and time. God had chosen to interrupt my life's plan "as is" and disengage my cruise control of singleness.

Our God is not "haphazard," blindly selecting and joining one with another. Our God is methodical, systematic, orderly and lovingly detailed with everything concerning us. God had chosen a seasoned educated intellectual with a generous heart who had a moral compass.

He was a confirmed bachelor with "no baby momma drama!" He loved children in spite of never fathering his own. He was cultured in performing arts, loved knowledge of learning into limitless subjects. This man read all sorts of literature. He was a scholar, and yes, truly a gentleman.

When the Lord presented him to me, it was absolutely difficult to accept him, simply because I was wholly, spiritually satisfied, married to the Lord. Isaiah 54:5 (KJV) "For thy Maker is thine husband; the Lord of hosts is his name; and thy Redeemer the Holy One of Israel; The God of the whole earth shall he be called."

Along with being solely focused upon my relationship with the Lord, the next question was, "Lord, does this man truly know you as his Lord and Savior?" This is when I understood where the kink in this man's armor was. He was a good man who needed a personal relationship with the Lord. My thoughts were, he needed salvation and time to grow spiritually. I would witness to him. That was it! I didn't have to get married! I could stay as I was, married to the Lord.

When we pray, the Lord has already searched our hearts for our truth for why we ask of Him for anything. Only the Lord knows our heart. Proverbs 21:2 (NIV) "A person may think their own ways are right, but the Lord weighs the heart." The Lord knew it would take great care to nurture a spiritual baby, as well as receive His choice of His expressed manifestation in a spouse. My praying turned into a 32 day fast before the Lord to have the assurance this man was God's choice and my husband. Early in the morning of day 32 of my fast, the Lord gave me a dream. The Lord and I were reasoning with one another. We were walking together on a path when I asked this question, "Lord, is he the one?" The Lord answered saying, John 3:16 (KJV) "For God so loved the world, that he gave his only begotten Son, that whosoever believeth in him should not perish, but have everlasting life." In essence, the Lord wanted me to receive His choice and that this man was the provision God had made for me. He would love me, and he was His only son that was meant to be my husband. With this assurance, I humbled myself and began our fellowship, friendship, courtship and his spiritual growth.

You see, before a vow is made at an altar with God and a spouse, a vow was made in our hearts to submit to God's selection for each other. There was also the understanding that the Spirit of the Lord spoke and reasoned with me first to nurture His man spiritually, to help him to arrive to Spiritual maturity, and that he was my husband. For the duration of our time of fellowship and as we grew together as a couple, I could not disclose to him that he was my husband. Since the Lord had revealed this to me, I knew it would be revealed to him in "God's timing."

We experienced highs and lows with communicating with each other. We worked at the same job site, but at different shifts. We didn't attend the same church and his spiritual growth was very slow at first. As a child, my husband attended church but had not received the Lord in his heart. He was religious and had only attended church very little as an adult. He was a good person but extremely carnal.

Let it be exposed now that during our courtship, we never engaged in sexual intercourse. This was battle ground Number #1, having the brother understand there would be no sex before marriage.

The Lord would allow the Word of God to resonate in his mind and spirit when it was reiterated in our conversations, when we would spend time together. In time we attended the same church with the same Bible teaching. This enabled us to understand the Word of God and grow spiritually balanced together. Also, the Lord had made me one of his primary "Bible Teachers." Hebrews 13:4 (KJV) "Marriage is honorable in all, and the bed undefiled: but whoremongers and adulterers God will judge." Hebrews 12:16 (NIV) "See that no one is sexually immoral, or is godless like Esau, who for a single meal sold his inheritance rights as the oldest son." 1 Corinthians 6:15-20 (KJV) "Know ye not that your bodies are the members of Christ? Shall I then take the members of Christ, and make them the members of an harlot? God forbid. What? Know ye not that he which is joined to an harlot is one body? For two, saith he, shall be one flesh. But he that is joined unto the Lord is one spirit. Flee fornication. Every sin that a man doeth is without the body; but he that committeth fornication sinneth against his own body. What? Know ye not that your body is the temple of the Holy Ghost, which is in you, which ye have of God, and ye are not your own? For ye are bought with a price: therefore glorify God in your body, and in your spirit, which are God's."

We had problems in our flesh and we both taught each other to respect each other. The more we observed each other in our local assembly, we became a part of the community spiritually. The accountability kept us both focused. I knew I had to pray more earnestly, for I had God's promise. He was my intended husband. The focus had to stay on the Lord with prayer when my flesh went to war with my spirit. 1 Corinthians 7:34 (KJV) "There is difference also between a wife and a virgin. The unmarried woman careth for the things of the Lord, that she may be holy both in body and in spirit: but she that is married careth for the things of the world, how she may please her husband."

We made it through this battle ground each time only because we loved the Lord more than we knew! Even though my husband was a babe in the Lord at the time, his ability to grow in self-discipline was a major advancement in his spiritual growth.

God was proving that His choice for a husband for me would benefit me later in ministry.

The next battle ground that was worked out in us was patience. When one is more spiritually mature than the other, you will need patience.

One of our first dates was spent at the public library. My husband was curious about my level of knowledge. He wanted to test what I knew. Men are intellectuals while women are largely emotional. He was pleasantly surprised on the various subjects he chose to question me on. His curiosity was satisfied. As a matter of fact, it seemed to spark in us both delight when we studied some subjects together. My husband has a wealth of knowledge and his capacity to retain information (to memory) is amazing. This quality of human knowledge was good, but God was testing us both. Now I had to have patience while God was dismantling his bride for his wealth of knowledge. He had to forsake the world's standard and approval of intellectual knowledge, the desire for my husband to develop a spiritual aptitude towards

God the Father. He needed to learn and put all his focus on knowing the Lord.

This is where we had our most trouble during our relationship. Before marriage, my husband relied heavily on his intellect.

He also had a hard time understanding how to let go of worldly activities that would compromise his Christian growth. This drove a wedge of separation between us periodically. I was watching for spiritual fruit to develop. Initially his spirituality was very slow.

He couldn't make the connect that everything about Christianity is spiritual.

Intellectually he was at an impasse with his Christian development and with me. These were the times I would remind God of His words in prayer for my intended husband.

The Lord was developing me in warring in the spirit for His man, to pray for his mind to turn away from the world and unto God. We have to trust God that men will do their part to make the transformation. Being equally yoked as believers and with one another is key! I had already been serving in ministry for some years at our local assembly. It was imperative to guard my heart and remain focused to the vocation God had given to me to stay effective. I would estrange myself from fellowship with him and pray to the Lord.

- Psalm 8:4-5 (NIV) "What is mankind that you are mindful of them, human beings that you care for them? You have made them[a] a little lower than the angels[b] and crowned them[c] with glory and honor."

- Philippians 2:5 (KJV) "Let this mind be in you, which was also in Christ Jesus."

- Romans 12:2 (KJV) "And be not conformed to this world: but be ye transformed by the renewing of your mind, that ye may prove what is that good, and acceptable, and perfect, will of God."

- Ephesians 5:17 (KJV) "Wherefore be ye not unwise but understanding what the will of the Lord is."

- Colossians 1:9-10 (KJV) "For this cause we also, since the day we heard it, do not cease to pray for you, and to desire that ye might be filled with knowledge of his will in all wisdom and spiritual understanding; that he might walk worthy of the Lord unto all pleasing, being fruitful in every good work, and increasing in the knowledge of God."

My life grew stronger and richer in the Word of God. My prayers for my husband drew me so much closer to the Lord, that I would not see my future husband in attendance in church. I would look over him intentionally and stay focused on serving in ministry. My husband had to realize that God had to be placed first in his life.

The Lord could not be an afterthought behind gratifying his flesh or the world. My husband began to realize, after a few times being shut out of fellowship, my going into consecration, and holding him accountable for his spiritual development, the change in him happened rapidly. He had to be firmly committed in his mind and heart to the Lord first before he could make a solemn committed vow to me.

During one of my consecrations that had been initially difficult to endure, I had grown to adore my husband's sweet mannerisms. The Holy Spirit whispered in my spirit during prayer on the altar in church, "Give him to me; I will return him to you!" That was the longest and last separation from each other. My husband truly began to grow and bear spiritual fruit. The Holy Spirit gave unto me a greater depth of trust in his ability to work within my future husband spiritually. He was becoming a man of God and not a religious follower of a denomination. When we returned to each other, we were both changed in our spirits. We praised God together with great joy in our hearts.

The Lord was knitting our souls together as one during our courtship.

God had presented me to my future husband at our work site. God had to deal with my heart with prayer and consecration to initially accept His man. I didn't know at that time it had been planted in his heart by his mother that it was time for him to get married. He had observed me for a period of six months from a distance at work. He watched how I carried myself with respect of myself and others. Our co-workers affectionately called me "Sister Good Book." I always made time to pray with those who asked. He noticed I wasn't intimidated with discussing scriptures with the men at work. I welcomed the dialogue. He had also observed that unexpectedly, I had to care for my granddaughter at work. He said I made a suddenly difficult situation appear seamlessly just another day on the job. He "watched" me as I made the day an adventure for my granddaughter until my daughter could get off work to pick her up. I never knew during that period of time he was observing me, that God had chosen his wife among all the rest. My husband never knew during our courtship that God told me he was in fact my husband. We both kept in our hearts the promises of God until he proposed publicly.

You see before vows are made, you are prepared to keep them no matter what. Especially if you are men and women of God. The Word of God teaches us, Ecclesiastes 5:4-5 (KJV) "When thou vowest a vow unto God, defer not to pay it; for he hath no pleasure in fools: pay that which thou hast vowed. Better is it that thou shouldest not vow, than that thou shouldest vow and not pay."

God teaches us by faith to stay true to Him with covenant. When we don't understand all about our God, we go to Him in fellowship for understanding and guidance to remain faithful to a loving God. We must also learn this in our marriage relationships with our spouse. The fellowship allows us to know and understand our spouse. Our vow to keep covenant with God and each other guards this trust we have in God for the keeping of our covenant vow. We can easily recognize motives and intents of one's heart when we spend quality time in each other's presence. We begin to appreciate each other's differences in how God knows uniquely the timing and suitability for all of us, especially when it comes to the sacrament of Holy matrimony.

We learn to observe, guard, protect, communicate, love and be vigilant before, during, and after our vows with pure motives. When times of testing come, we pray for the Lord to anchor our souls during our storms of life. Hebrews 6:19-20 (KJV) "Which hope we have as an anchor of the soul, both sure and stedfast, and which entereth into that within the veil; Whither the forerunner is for us entered, even Jesus, made a high priest for ever after the order of Melchisedec."

The Lord Jesus Christ is the only one that can help us keep our marriages on the right course together. When we have been challenged, we don't give up and fall out of marriage. We give into prayer and fall on our knees. We thank the Lord for each other "as is." We don't have a perfect marriage by no means. What we do have is a covenant agreement with God and it's binding. We are committed to prayer, patience, and waiting to hear from God, when we find each other difficult to understand.

We had a long courtship and we have been married for some years now. I've learned to observe my husband very well, to know when to allow my husband to nurture his own fellowship with the Lord. He faithfully serves in ministry and studies God's Word at his own pace. He is a strong supporter always as I minister the gospel of Jesus Christ. He is my "Lapidoth and I am his Deborah." I have always told my husband; he knows how to handle this Woman of God with a "fiery spirit!" My husband has an even temperament and has studied me well enough to know me. I thank God for all his observations.

If I could leave one piece of helpful information before taking your vows, it would be this: Women don't be desperate for a husband. Men make sure you observe and inquire of God before you approach a woman with the expectation of marriage. Realize that your value and worth as women and men of God is of great value! You will both have praise of God all the days of your lives!

Proverbs 31:10-12 (KJV) "Who can find a virtuous woman? For her price is far above rubies. The heart of her husband doth safely trust in her, so that he shall have no need of spoil. She will do him good and not evil all the days of her life."

May peace by your journey in Jesus Name. Dr. Karen Amos, D.TH

Resources: Books

- The Rules of Engagement: The Art of Strategic Prayer and Spiritual Warfare, by Dr. Cindy Trimm

- The Believers Authority, by Kenneth Hagin, Sr.

- The Power of a Praying Wife, by Stormie Omartain The Battlefield of the Mind, by Joyce Meyers Nothing Just Happens, by T. D. Jakes

Scriptures

(1 Corinthians 15:55-57 NKJV) ""O[a] Death, where is your sting? O Hades, where is your victory?" The sting of death is sin, and the strength of sin is the law. But thanks be to God, who gives us the victory through our Lord Jesus Christ."

(1 Corinthians 6:15-20 KJV) "Know ye not that your bodies are the members of Christ? shall I then take the members of Christ, and make them the members of a harlot? God forbid. What? know ye not that he which is joined to a harlot is one body? for two, saith he, shall be one flesh. But he that is joined unto the Lord is one spirit. Flee fornication. Every sin that a man doeth is without the body; but he that committeth fornication sinneth against his own body.

What? know ye not that your body is the temple of the Holy Ghost, which is in you, which ye have of God, and ye are not your own? For ye are bought with a price: therefore glorify God in your body, and in your spirit, which are God's."

(1 Corinthians 7:34 KJV) "There is difference also between a wife and a virgin. The unmarried woman careth for the things of the Lord, that she may be holy both in body and in spirit: but she that is married careth for the things of the world, how she may please her husband."

(1 Corinthians 13:13 NIV) "And now these three remain: faith, hope and love. But the greatest of these is love."

(1 Corinthians 15:55 NKJV) "O Death, where is your sting? O Hades, where is your victory?" The sting of death is sin, and the strength of sin is the law. But thanks be to God, who gives us the victory through our Lord Jesus Christ."

(1 Corinthians 15:57 NKJV) "But thanks be to God! He gives us the victory through our Lord Jesus Christ."

(1 John 4:4 ESV) "for he who is in you is greater than he who is in the world.

(1 Thessalonians 5:16-18 NIV) "Always be joyful. Never stop praying. Be thankful in all circumstances,

for this is God's will for you who belong to Christ Jesus."

(Daniel 3:25 NLT) ""Look!" Nebuchadnezzar shouted. "I see four men, unbound, walking around in the fire unharmed! And the fourth looks like a god[a]!"

(Ecclesiastes 4:12 NIV) "Though one may be overpowered, two can defend themselves. A cord of three strands is not quickly broken."

(Ephesians 5:17 KJV) "Wherefore be ye not unwise but understanding what the will of the Lord is."

(Ephesians 5:21-24 NLT) "And further, submit to one another out of reverence for Christ. For wives, this means submit to your husbands as to the Lord. For a husband is the head of his wife as Christ is the head of the church. He is the Savior of his body, the church. As the church submits to Christ, so you wives should submit to your husbands in everything."

(Ephesians 6:10-12 NIV) "Finally, be strong in the Lord and in his mighty power. Put on the full armor of God, so that you can take your stand against the devil's schemes. For our struggle is not against flesh and blood, but against the rulers, against the authorities, against the powers of this dark world and against the spiritual forces of evil in the heavenly realms."

(Ephesians 6:11 ESV) "Put on the whole armor of God, that you may be able to stand against the schemes of the devil."

(Ephesians 6:12 NIV) "For our struggle is not against flesh and blood, but against the rulers, against the authorities, against the powers of this dark world and against the spiritual forces of evil in the heavenly realms."

(Ephesians 6:12 NLT) "For we are not fighting against flesh-and- blood enemies, but against evil rulers and authorities of the unseen world, against mighty powers in this dark world, and against evil spirits in the heavenly places."

(Ephesians 6:13-14 KJV) "Wherefore take unto you the whole armour of God, that ye may be able to withstand in the evil day, and having done all, to stand. Stand therefore, having your loins girt about with truth, and having on the breastplate of righteousness;"

(Galatians 1:5 NKJV) "to whom be glory forever and ever."

(Genesis 2:24 NKJV) "Therefore a man shall leave his father and mother and be joined to his wife, and they shall become one flesh."

(Hebrews 11:1-2 NIV) "Faith shows the reality of what we hope for; it is the evidence of things we cannot see. Through their faith, the people in days of old earned a good reputation."

(Hebrews 13:4 KJV) "Marriage is honourable in all, and the bed undefiled: but whoremongers and adulterers God will judge."

(Hebrews 13:5 NKJV) "Let your conduct be without covetousness; be content with such things as you have. For He Himself has said, "I will never leave you nor forsake you."

(Isaiah 9:1 NLT) "Nevertheless, that time of darkness and despair will not go on forever."(Isaiah

26:3 NKJV) "You will keep him in perfect peace, Whose mind is stayed on You, Because he trusts in You."

(Isaiah 32:18 KJV) "And my people shall dwell in a peaceable habitation, and in sure dwellings, and in quiet resting places;"

(Isaiah 53:5 KJV) "But he was wounded for our transgressions, he was bruised for our iniquities: the chastisement of our peace was upon him; and with

his stripes we are healed."

(Isaiah 54:5 KJV) "For thy Maker is thine husband; the Lord of hosts is his name; and thy Redeemer the Holy One of Israel; The God of the whole earth shall he be called."

(Isaiah 54:17 KJV) "No weapon that is formed

against thee shall prosper; and every tongue that shall rise against thee in judgment thou shalt condemn. This is the heritage of the servants of the Lord, and their righteousness is of me, saith the Lord."

(Isaiah 61:3 KJV) "To appoint unto them that mourn in Zion, to give unto them beauty for ashes, the oil of joy for mourning, the garment of praise for the spirit of heaviness; that they might be called trees of righteousness, the planting of the Lord, that he might be glorified."

(Jeremiah 29:11 KJV) "For I know the thoughts that I think toward you, saith the Lord, thoughts of peace, and not of evil, to give you an expected end."

(Jeremiah 29:11 BSB) "For I know the plans I have for you, declares the LORD, plans to prosper you and not to harm you, to give you a future and a hope."

(John 3:16 KJV) "For God so loved the world, that he gave his only begotten Son, that whosoever believeth in him should not perish, but have everlasting life."

136

(John 8:44 NKJV) "You are of your father the devil, and the desires of your father you want to do. He was a murderer from the beginning, and does not stand in the truth, because there is no truth in him. When he speaks a lie, he speaks from his own resources, for he is a liar and the father of it."

(Matthew 18:20 NIV) "For where two or three gather together as my followers, [a] I am there among them."

(Philippians 1:6 NASB) "For I am confident of this very thing, that He who began a good work in you will perfect it until the day of Christ Jesus."

(Philippians 2:5 KJV) "Let this mind be in you, which was also in Christ Jesus:"

(Proverbs 3:5-6 NIV) "Trust in the LORD with all your heart; do not depend on your own understanding. Seek his will in all you do, and he will show you which path to take."

(Proverbs 21:2 NIV) "A person may think their own

ways are right, but the LORD weighs the heart."

(Proverbs 31:10-12 KJV) "Who can find a virtuous woman? for her price is far above rubies. The heart of her husband doth safely trust in her, so that he shall have no need of spoil. She will do him good and not evil all the days of her life."

(Psalm 8:4-5 NIV) "what is mankind that you are mindful of them, human beings that you care for them? [a] You have made them[b] a little lower than the angels[c] and crowned them[d] with glory and honor."

(Psalm 5:11-12 KJV) "But let all those that put their trust in thee rejoice; let them ever shout for joy, because thou defendest them: let them also that love thy name be joyful in thee. For thou, LORD, wilt bless the righteous; with favour wilt thou compass him as with a shield."

(Psalm 18:2) "The Lord is my rock and my fortress and my deliverer; My God, my [a]strength, in whom I will trust; My shield and the [b]horn of my salvation, my stronghold."

(Psalm 23 NIV) "The Lord is my shepherd; I have all that I need. He lets me rest in green meadows; he leads me beside peaceful streams. He renews my strength. He guides me along right paths, bringing honor to his name. Even when I walk through the darkest valley, [a] I will not be afraid, for you are close beside me. Your rod and your staff protect and comfort me. You prepare a feast for me in the presence of my enemies. You honor me by anointing my head with oil. My cup overflows with blessings. Surely your goodness and unfailing love will pursue me all the days of my life, and I will live in the house of the Lord forever."

(Psalm 23:5 KJV) "Lord, you prepare a table before

me in the presence of my enemies. You anoint my head with oil; my cup overflows."

(Psalm 23:5 NKJV) "You prepare a table before me in the presence of my enemies; You anoint my head with oil; My cup runs over."

(Psalm 30:5 NIV) "For his anger lasts only a moment, but his favor lasts a lifetime; weeping may stay for the night, but rejoicing comes in the morning."

(Psalm 51:10) "Create in me a clean heart, O God. Renew a loyal spirit within me."

(Psalm 61:2 NKJV) "Lead me to the rock that is higher than I."

(Psalm 91:1-7 KJV) "He that dwelleth in the secret place of the most High shall abide under the shadow of the Almighty. I will say of the Lord, He is my refuge and my fortress: my God; in him will I trust. Surely he shall deliver thee from the snare of the fowler, and from the noisome pestilence. He shall cover thee with his feathers, and under his wings shalt thou trust: his truth shall be thy shield and buckler. Thou shalt not be afraid for the terror by night; nor for the arrow that flieth by day; Nor for the pestilence that walketh in darkness; nor for the destruction that wasteth at noonday. A thousand shall fall at thy side, and ten thousand at thy right hand; but it shall not come nigh thee."

(Psalm 121:4 NIV) "indeed, he who watches over Israel will neither slumber nor sleep."

(Revelation 12:11 NKJV) "And they overcame him by the blood of the Lamb and by the word of their testimony, and they did not love their lives to the death."

(Revelation 12:11 NIV) "They triumphed over him by the blood of the Lamb and by the word of their testimony; they did not love their lives so much as to shrink from death."

(Romans 8:1 KJV) "There is therefore now no condemnation to them which are in Christ Jesus, who walk not after the flesh, but after the Spirit."

(Romans 8:28 KJV) "And we know that all things work together for good to them that love God, to them who are the called according to his purpose."

(Romans 12:2 KJV) "And be not conformed to this world: but be ye transformed by the renewing of your mind, that ye may prove what is that good, and acceptable, and perfect, will of God."

About The Authors

Cantres Clark is a prophetic intercessor and lover of Jesus Christ! She is a San Francisco Bay Area native who is happily married to her husband of two decades. She is the mother of two amazing teenagers. Cantres is passionate about evangelizing the healing power of prayer and worship to those who have an ear to hear. She is inspired by the beautiful things of God and delights in writing love poems about His splendor. She enjoys adventures and aspires to witness God's Seven Natural Wonders of the world through international travel.

Throughout her multifaceted career as a mental health practitioner and an entrepreneur, she has provided guidance to hundreds of individuals who have endured emotional and financial hardship. In 2020, upon completion of her PhD in Trauma Therapy and Epidemiology, Cantres will release her first solo work, *The Cross, The Sword, and a Stick, Overcoming Demonic Attacks.* To learn more, visit Worshipyourwayout.com

Mary Jones-Lofton is a native of Vallejo, California. She is currently employed with Hospital Corporations of America (HCA) as a Market Operations Manager. She holds a Bachelor of Business Studies in Management, a Master of Arts in Healthcare Management, and a Master of Business Administration in Healthcare Management. Mary has been married for over 34 years and has one son and one daughter. Her purpose for writing *Before the Vow Breaks* is to encourage wives to not give up on praying for their marriage and to trust that God has a strategy to bring His purpose to pass no matter how impossible the situation appears to be. Her mission is to be in God's Will and to make an impact through the power of prayer. For more information, contact Mary at mlofton@swbell.net

Jean Burns was born in New Orleans, Louisiana. She is a wife and phenomenal mother to three amazing angelic children. She currently resides in the beautiful city of Brentwood, California. She attends part-time online courses at Regent University where she is obtaining her bachelor's degree in Psychology. She is also a full-time student at Contra Costa Medical Career College obtaining her Sterile Processing Technician certification. She also aspires to write her own best-seller book. In her spare time, she loves to sing, write poetry and journal. She also loves to garden, take long walks and mediate. She has a passion for life coaching and motivational speaking. She focuses on self-love and encourages many people to step out into their true potential. She is heavily armored with the breastplate of righteousness, feet shod with preparation and the sword of the spirit/Word of God. For more information, contact Jean at jeanburns11@yahoo.com

Cynthia Jackson accepted her call to ministry in January 1992 and she was licensed and ordained 1997 under Dr. Willie T. Gaines at the Emmanuel Baptist Church in San Jose, CA. She has since served under Dr. Alan Ragland – Third Baptist Church of Chicago and Pastor Horacio Jones, Family Bible Fellowship (FBF). She is a respected Bible teacher, preacher and prayer warrior. She holds graduate and undergraduate degrees and is a certified facilitator. In February of 2003, Cynthia accepted the call to full-time ministry and served at FBF.

In 2007 God would call her to birth Transformed Through Hope Ministries in which she and her husband co-pastor. Her favorite scripture is Philippians 4:13, *I can do all things through Christ, which strengthens me.*

She is the wife of Pastor Wayne D. Jackson. They are blessed with two sons, Andre and Anthone, one daughter in love (Ashlee), and soon will welcome the third grandchild. Learn more at www. transformedthroughhope.org

Jennifer James-Lewis currently works for Stockton Unified School District. She has been working in the early childhood field for 25 years. She is a graduate of Contra Costa College with an associate degree in Liberal Arts in Science. She also has a bachelor's degree in Psychology. She graduated from University of Phoenix. She is a wife and has been married for three years to Roderick Lewis. Jennifer currently attends Hope Center in Merced, California, under Pastors Darryl and Christiane Robinson. She teaches children's ministry. Jennifer enjoys teaching to the children because they are the future. Jennifer is over Jubilee Christian Book Club. She gets together with people to discuss various books and gives knowledge and insight, which helps their lives. Jennifer has a passion to help people. Her favorite scripture is Hebrews 11:1, *Now faith is confidence in what we hope for and assurance about what we do not see.* For more information, contact Jennifer at skreen79894@aol.com.

Dr. Karen Amos is a faithful and committed member of Acts Full Gospel Church, Oakland, CA, under the leadership of Bishop Bob Jackson, where she currently serves as Sunday School Superintendent of Religious Education. She has a passion for the teaching ministry and has effectively led the Religious Educators to higher dimensions. Dr. Amos has dedicated her life to humbly serve the Lord Jesus Christ by leading others into the Kingdom of God through evangelism, witnessing and biblical truths for Christian Living. Dr. Amos is an avid learner. She is a Professor of Biblical Studies, holding a bachelor's degree in Biblical Studies, a master's degree in Christian Counseling, a master's degree in Theology and a Doctorate Degree in Theology. In 2018 she was awarded an Honorary Doctorate Degree of Humanity.

Dr. Amos is a loving mother of one daughter, and a devoted grandmother of four. She has recently celebrated five years of marital bliss with her husband, Will Amos, who is a mighty man of God and pillar of support to Dr. Amos' commissioned call upon her life. Dr. Amos is a Holy Spirit led Woman of God, walking in her purpose, while confessing *I press on toward the goal to win the prize of God's Heavenly calling in Christ Jesus* (Philippians 3:14). Contact Info: drkamos8@gmail.com

Denise Smith *(Visionary Author)* believes in the POWER of prayer and has made it her mission to engage, equip, encourage and empower wives to believe in the POWER of prayer as well. She knows that as a wife, God has called her to be her husband's helper (Genesis 2:18), to aid and assist and to be his strong defender and warrior in the physical and spiritual battles of life.

Denise lives with her husband Lonnie, in Antioch, California. Together they have 6 sons, and 5 grandchildren (3 girls and 2 boys). In addition to her being a strong defender and warrior (prayer), she enjoys worshiping through song, working out, traveling and spending time with her family.

To learn more, visit www.wiveswhowar.com. You may also join the Wives Who War community on Facebook at https://www.facebook. com/groups/WivesWhoWar/

Dortha L. Hise (*Visionary Author*) is the owner of a full-service multi-virtual assistant company specializing in untangling tech for their overwhelmed clients and the creator of On the Healing Path with Dortha, which is a community where people come together to share how they use nature for healing. Dortha believes in the healing power of prayer and spending time nature to spend time with God. After enduring the loss of 28 people during a 2-year period, Dortha really connected to her faith and deepened her relationship with God learning about the healing power of nature while on a backpacking trip on the Pacific Crest Trail in Northern California. Dortha knew that she was meant to share her story to help others to do the same.

Dortha currently lives with her husband Jason, in Folsom, California. They have 2 feathered babies, Chuck and Nunchuck. In addition to being a prayer warrior, she enjoys working out, hiking, and time with family and friends.

Learn more at https://prettysmartvaservices.com/ and join the healing community https://www.facebook.com/groups/622122965046442/